I0015608

Gamefroot   Table of Contents – 2017 Edition

Learn tomorrow skills TODAY

with TomorrowSKILLS.COM

License Agreement

This book (the "Book") is a product provided by HobbyPRESS (being referred to as "HobbyPRESS" in this document), subject to your compliance with the terms and conditions set forth below. PLEASE READ THIS DOCUMENT CAREFULLY BEFORE ACCESSING OR USING THE BOOK. BY ACCESSING OR USING THE BOOK, YOU AGREE TO BE BOUND BY THE TERMS AND CONDITIONS SET FORTH BELOW. IF YOU DO NOT WISH TO BE BOUND BY THESE TERMS AND CONDITIONS, YOU MAY NOT ACCESS OR USE THE BOOK. HOBBYPRESS MAY MODIFY THIS AGREEMENT AT ANY TIME, AND SUCH MODIFICATIONS SHALL BE EFFECTIVE IMMEDIATELY UPON POSTING OF THE MODIFIED AGREEMENT ON THE CORPORATE SITE OF HOBBYPRESS. YOU AGREE TO REVIEW THE AGREEMENT PERIODICALLY TO BE AWARE OF SUCH MODIFICATIONS AND YOUR CONTINUED ACCESS OR USE OF THE BOOK SHALL BE DEEMED YOUR CONCLUSIVE ACCEPTANCE OF THE MODIFIED AGREEMENT.

Restrictions on Alteration

You may not modify the Book or create any derivative work of the Book or its accompanying documentation.   Derivative works include but are not limited to translations.

Restrictions on Copying

You may not copy any part of the Book unless formal written authorization is obtained from us.

Limitation of Liability

HobbyPRESS will not be held liable for any advice or suggestions given in this book. If the reader wants to follow a suggestion, it is at his or her own discretion. Suggestions are only offered to help.

IN NO EVENT WILL HOBBYPRESS BE LIABLE FOR (I) ANY INCIDENTAL, CONSEQUENTIAL, OR INDIRECT DAMAGES (INCLUDING, BUT NOT LIMITED TO, DAMAGES FOR LOSS OF PROFITS, BUSINESS INTERRUPTION, LOSS OF PROGRAMS OR INFORMATION, AND THE LIKE) ARISING OUT OF THE USE OF OR INABILITY TO USE THE BOOK. EVEN IF HOBBYPRESS OR ITS AUTHORIZED REPRESENTATIVES HAVE BEEN ADVISED OF THE POSSIBILITY OF SUCH DAMAGES, OR (II) ANY CLAIM ATTRIBUTABLE TO ERRORS, OMISSIONS, OR OTHER INACCURACIES IN THE BOOK. You agree to indemnify, defend and hold harmless HobbyPRESS, its officers, directors, employees, agents, licensors, suppliers and any third party information providers to the Book from and against all losses, expenses, damages and costs, including reasonable attorneys' fees, resulting from any violation of this Agreement (including negligent or wrongful conduct) by you or any other person using the Book.

Miscellaneous

This Agreement shall all be governed and construed in accordance with the laws of Hong Kong applicable to agreements made and to be performed in Hong Kong. You agree that any legal action or proceeding between HobbyPRESS and you for any purpose concerning this Agreement or the parties' obligations hereunder shall be brought exclusively in a court of competent jurisdiction sitting in Hong Kong.

About the TomorrowSKILLS Series

Give yourself a strong head start in computer programming with our TomorrowSKILLS books, which are published fresh in 2017. Through these books you will learn how programming works and how simple programs may be created using ready-made resources and modern drag-and-drop programming environments.

We use Gamefroot version 2.4 for demo purpose. Gamefroot is a drag and drop program design environment which also allows visual programming. Visual programming involves dragging objects or components. Simply put, you don't type codes - you drag and drop codes!

Basic Requirements

We assume you are totally new to programming. To make things easy for you, we use simple language throughout the book. And we simplify many of the technical terms into something more straight forward and human friendly. Most trade jargons are intentionally skipped.

This is an easy-read book that attempts to make concepts SIMPLE and STRAIGHTFORWARD. It does not aim to cover everything in Gamefroot. It simply tries to get you started quickly.

You need to be computer literate. You should know how to use a web browser since Gamefroot is web based. And you should have a reasonably configured computer system that comes with a dual core processor, 2GB+ of RAM, several GBs of free drive space that hold the resource files, and an active internet connection ... etc.

As of the time of this writing the latest version of Gamefroot is 2.4.

About Gamefroot

Gamefroot is the world's easiest to use game creator and allow's you to fast track your web and mobile game development! Gamefroot games are now powered by our own HTML5 game engine

Version 2.4

- Templates should be quicker and better.
- Pro and Educational accounts are now 'live'.
- You can now export to IOS and Android.
- A few User Experience changes in the Asset Palette making nicer animations.
- In the Asset Manager we have change the order in which packs are displayed, making it easier to manage your packs.
- A dropdown in the Resources sidebar, making it easier to go through a resource.

Version 2.3

- You can now duplicate levels.
- Changes to templates, making it easier for users.

You need a proper web browser. The latest version of Chrome is recommended. You need to login to use Gamefroot. If you have a google/FB account, you do not need to separately open an account. Otherwise you must first create an account.

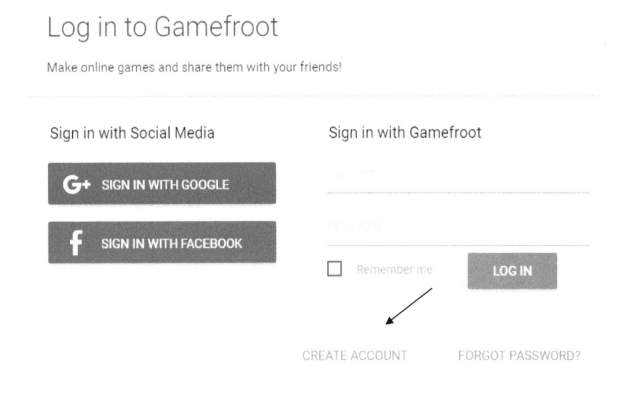

Log in to Gamefroot

Make online games and share them with your friends!

Sign in with Social Media

G+ SIGN IN WITH GOOGLE

f SIGN IN WITH FACEBOOK

Sign in with Gamefroot

☐ Remember me   **LOG IN**

CREATE ACCOUNT   FORGOT PASSWORD?

To get started you may choose an option from the opening screen. For learning purpose, you should start with a blank template.

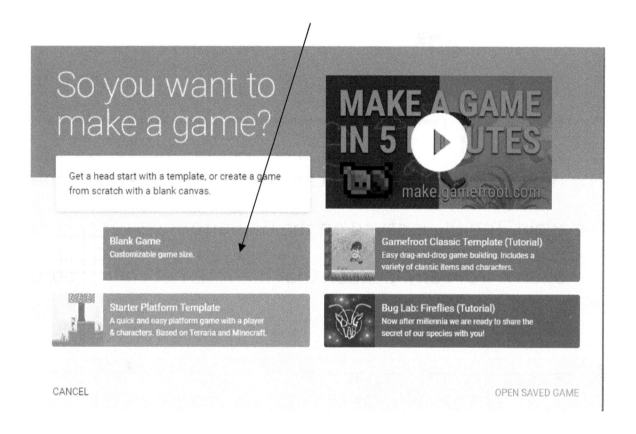

The File menu has options to save the game. All you need is to provide a name for the game.

The next time you login you can always open up the game file again. The file is saved on the Gamefroot server so you can open it from any location that has internet connection.

Learning Goals

In a modern software development venture there are 3 different roles. Designers plan the program flow and conceptualize the various program features. Artists draw the user interface elements and the surrounding environment so to create the look and feel of the program. Programmers implement the design accordingly by writing codes. This book teaches you the basics of block based programming using Gamefroot. You will assume the role of a programmer and also a designer. And you will learn to use ready-made components from templates and/or other opensource resources to speed up the software creation process.

The Gamefroot interface allows you to code and then play

the result directly by pressing the Play button. This is extremely useful for learning the essential programming concepts and logics:

The Script Editor is for coding.

Assets are game resources.

Play lets you see the result immediately.

Visual programming involves creating computer program using pictorial elements. Gamefroot is special in that apart from drag and drop it also offers a block based script editor – you drag and drop code blocks to form a program.

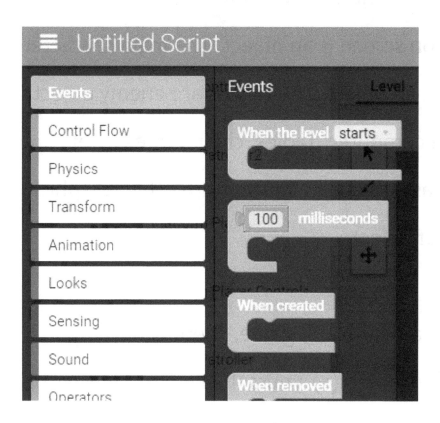

Lesson 1 - the concept of game objects

The first thing we want you to know is that everything that gets shown on screen is an object. The main character that you control is an object. The villains are enemy objects controlled by the computer. Tables, chairs, trees ... etc are all considered as objects. Sprites are the graphical representations of objects.

When you create a new blank game, there is nothing in it and you must add object(s) yourself. For a game to be functional there has to be at least one object on screen!

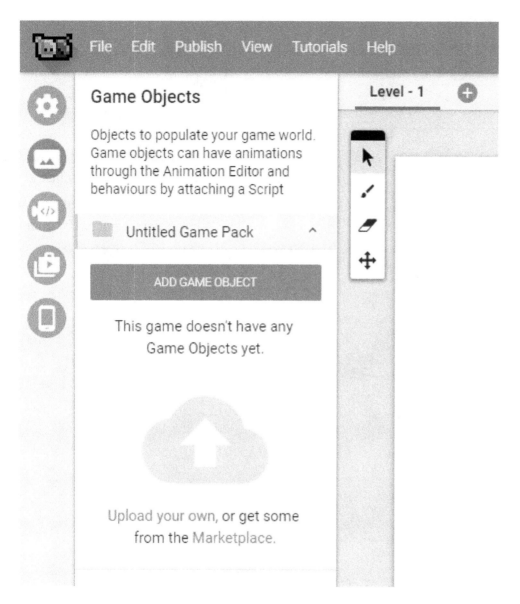

You may upload an existing object from your computer, or you may call up the Character Creator, which allows you to assemble new character object using existing body parts.

You may upload existing graphics.

You simply point and click to choose body parts. You need to click Save Character for your creation to be usable.

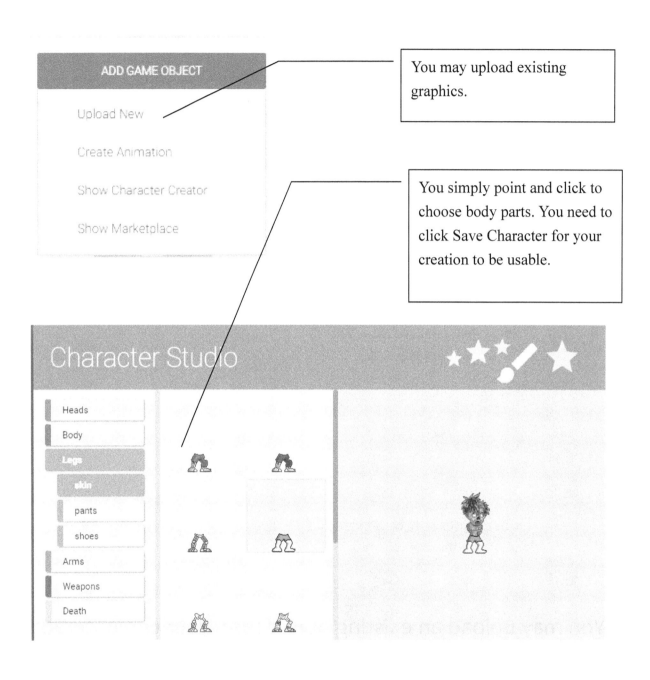

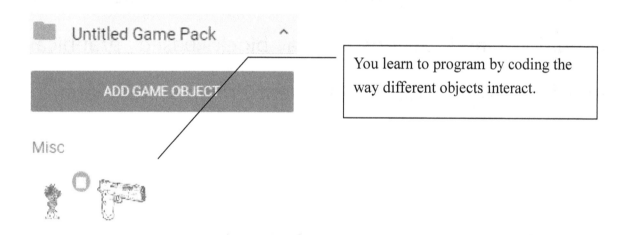

Upload Game Objects

Select image files from your computer to upload as Game Objects

Most of the popular graphic file formats are supported.

Click Add Files to upload.

Untitled Game Pack

ADD GAME OBJECT

You learn to program by coding the way different objects interact.

Misc

Gamefroot is object oriented. Every item that shows up in

the game is an object. Every object has a set of properties

which represent the object's unique characteristics. They can be predefined, and some may even be manipulated At runtime through event triggered actions.

Even though Gamefroot works as a visual block based tool, its core is no different from a traditional object oriented development system. It is fully event driven, and the only difference is that you may define the various event conditions and actions via a block based graphical interface. We will talk about event driven system later in this book.

It is good to have quality graphics and sound effects for enriching your game. OpenGameArt (http://opengameart.org) provides thousands of public domain game arts and sound effects that are completely free to use in your game. Free artworks for games are typically offered as sprites and backdrops in JPG or PNG format. Sprites are for foreground objects while backdrops are for the background. They are usually made available in the form of sprite sheets so you can freely copy and paste.

Character sprites and tiles: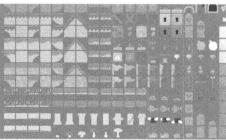

You may also use resources from the marketplace. We will talk about this later.

Lesson 1 – more on game objects

You can drag and drop to place game objects onto the level editor. You can drag the corners of the object to resize as needed (a more flexible way of resizing a sprite is through coding – we will talk about this later).

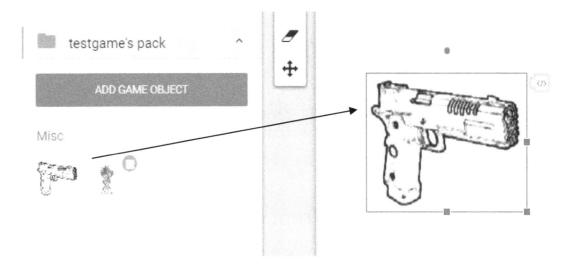

An object by itself does not do anything. You need to add script to it to tell what should be done. You can always right click on the object and choose Add script.

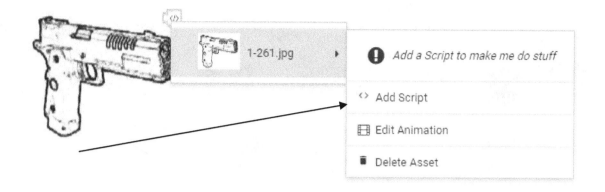

When you click Add script you will switch to the script editor mode which allows you to do block based programming.

Frame is a different concept. A frame is a graphical representation of an object, sort of like a sprite. When there are multiple frames, an animation sequence is formed, which makes the object kind of animated. You can right click on an object to set or modify its animation sequence.

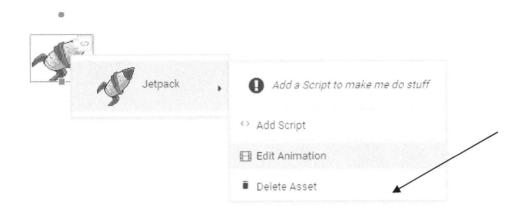

You need to give the animation sequence a unique name. The sequence can contain one or more frames. Generally, more frames means smoother animation.

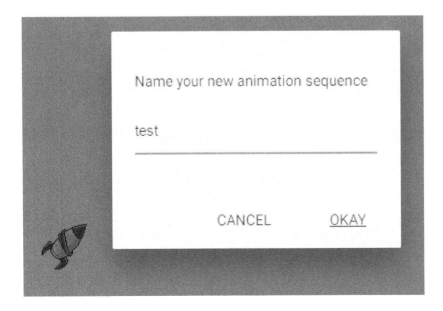

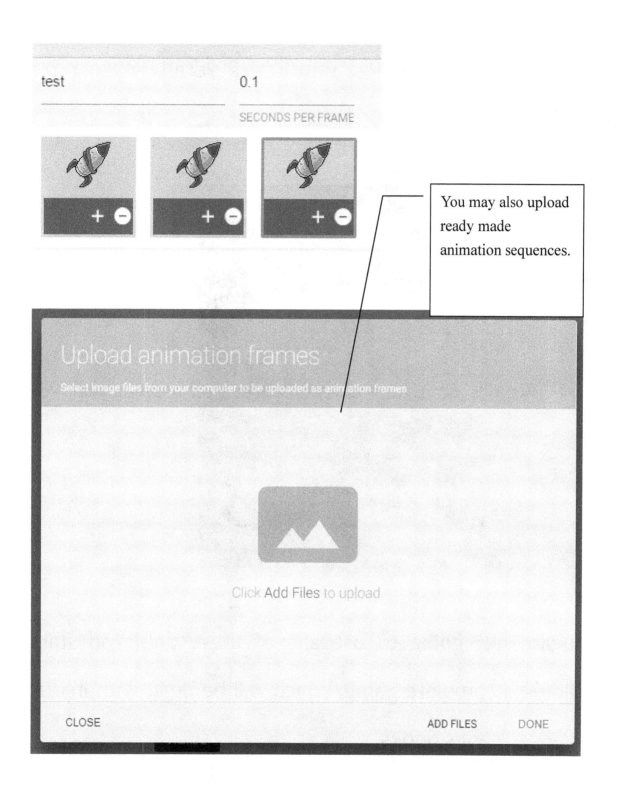

You may also upload ready made animation sequences.

Copyright   2017   **The HobbyPRESS (Hong Kong)**.

Object animation can be controlled programmatically via these code blocks:

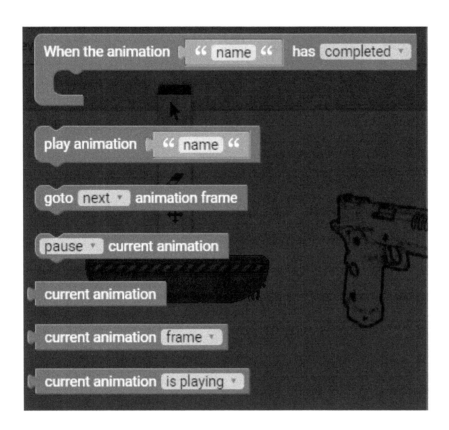

You are not going to use any of these until you start building a complete game, which will be dealt with in our advanced series books.

Hitbox is a boundary box for the object. It can be used to detect collision. The default is a square shape box. You can customize the boundaries on a frame by frame basis. Normally you can leave the default hitbox settings unchanged.

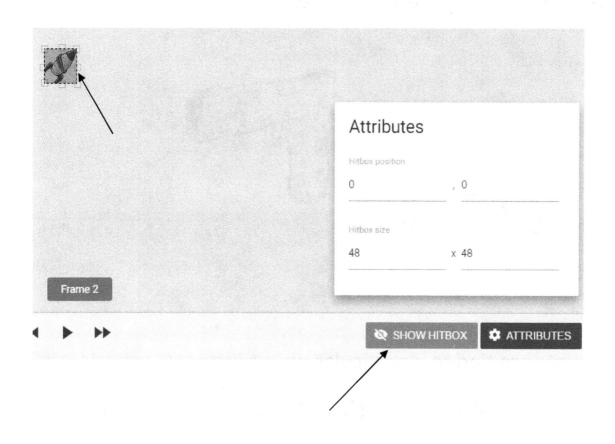

Lesson 1 con't – object instances

In theory the same object can be added into the same level multiple times. By doing this you end up having multiple instances of the same object. The original object becomes sort of like a template.

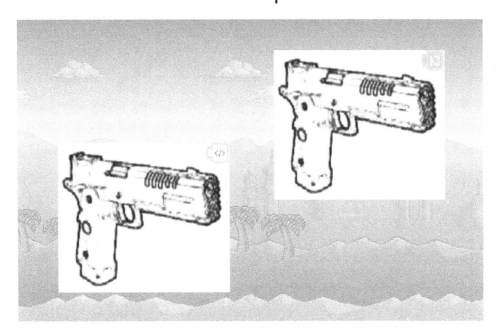

Scripts are tied to a particular object instance. Instances of the same object do not share the same scripts by default. To allow other instances to use the same script, you click on the script and then click on these object instances one by one. The little icon on the upper right corner of the object instance will get filled up.

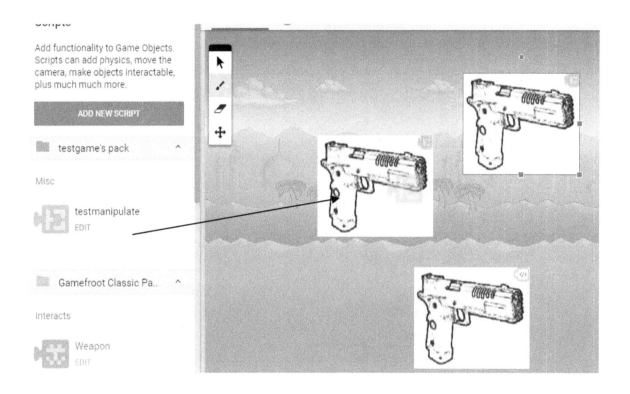

Keep in mind, when they are sharing the same script, any modifications you made through one of them will get reflected on all of them.

To avoid confusion and for simplicity sake, we do NOT recommend that you work with multiple instances of the same object. At the beginner level you should skip this and focus on basic coding concepts.

To remove unnecessary objects from screen, right click and choose Delete Asset.

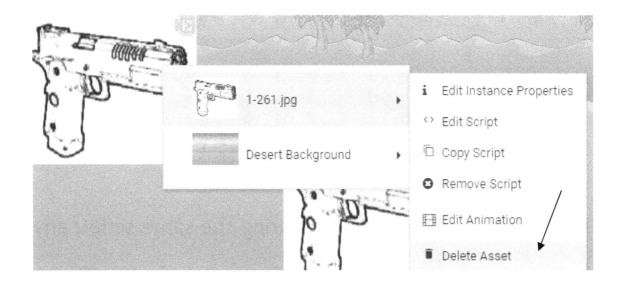

Lesson 1 con't – levels, layers, tiles, terrain, background and camera

The level is where the objects are acting. After placing the necessary objects on the level, you define their basic behaviors through code blocks. Level properties is where you define the size of the level (the world size). You can even pick a background color for it. For learning purpose you can keep the default values.

Level Properties

Level Name

Level - 1

World Size

x: 2880   y: 2880

Background Color

🎨 SET COLOUR

Layer is a different concept. If you have experience using Photoshop or other Paint programs you should know what layers are for.

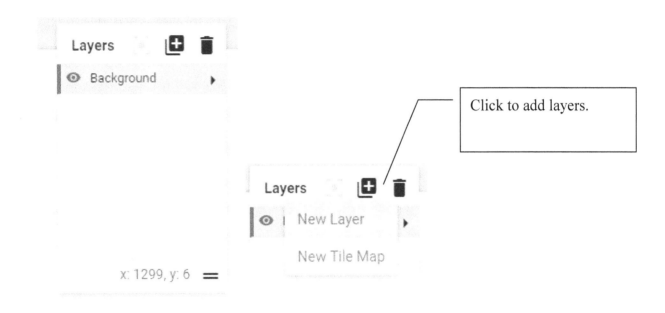

Click to add layers.

A layer is a component in a complex level. Think of it as a set of transparencies that are stacked on top of each other. Each layer contains part of the level. One layer might have the background. One might have the main character object. Another might display the energy bars. When working, you can view each layer by itself, or you can stack the layers on top of one another and view the stack as one level. Each level can have one or more layers. When the game is being played, all layers are automatically combined. Such mechanism can be very useful because it allows you to move and manipulate parts of a level to see how your changes are going to affect the whole level.

It is always a good practice to have a separate layer for your game objects. You can give the new layer a meaningful name.

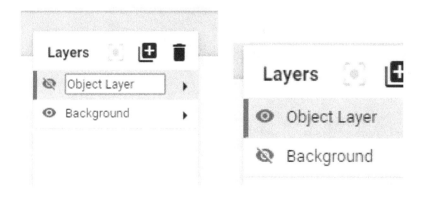

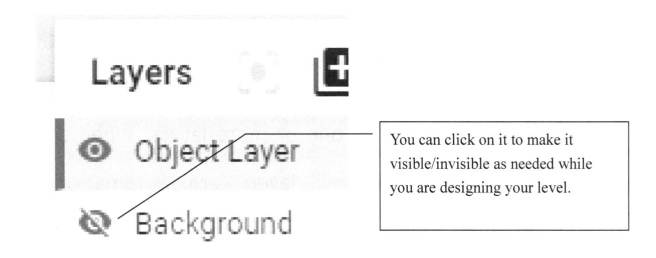

You can click on it to make it visible/invisible as needed while you are designing your level.

Background is not the same as layer. In Gamefroot, background related stuff can be referred to as terrain or tile set. They should be placed in a separate tile map layer.

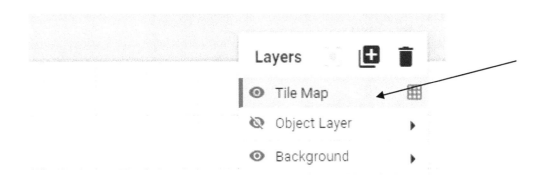

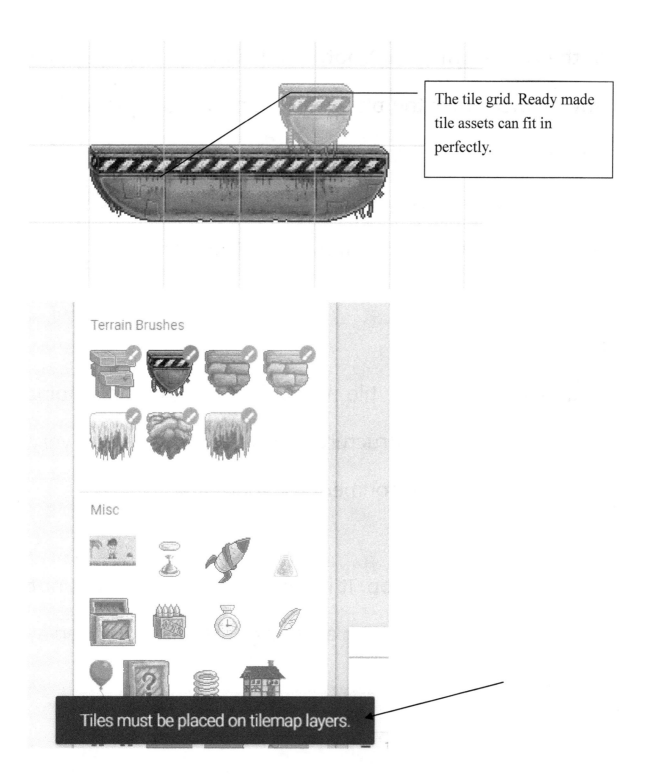

The tile grid. Ready made tile assets can fit in perfectly.

Terrain Brushes

Misc

Tiles must be placed on tilemap layers.

In the context of Gamefroot, terrain is what makes up the environment that the player object moves around in. The tile map layer (the layer with grids) serves as the layer for terrain. Tiles are sized/resized and arranged in the tile map and are solid and non-movable. They are NOT even scriptable.

You place tiles on the tile map grid through simple point and click. Properly structured tiles can assemble a very nice background environment for your game.

Background is backdrop. It is behind everything and is not capable of interacting with anything. It should be placed at the Background layer.

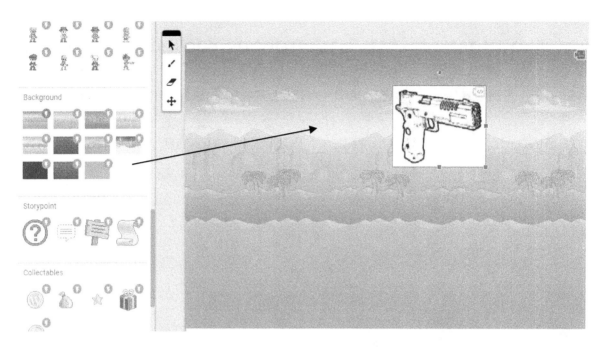

It is technically possible to place multiple background images on the same background layer.

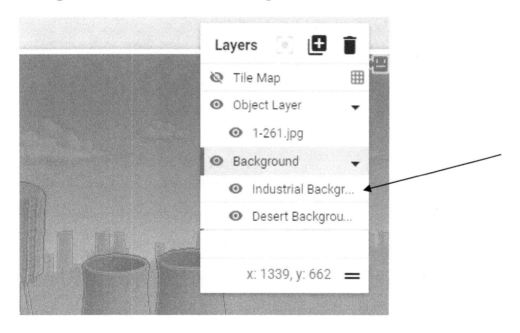

just like other objects, backgrounds can be manipulated using scripts. The backgrounds supplied by the ready-made assets pack often come with some pre-defined scripts.

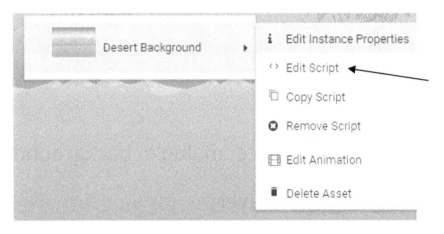

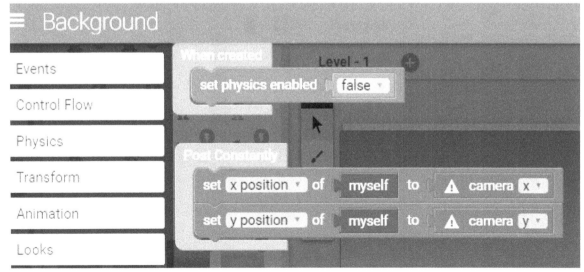

If you do not like to use any background, you can keep the

background as blank, and set a color for it.

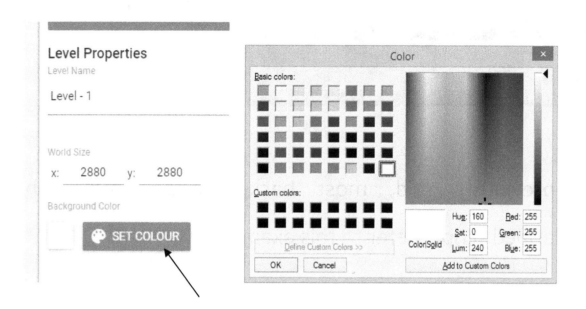

Camera is sort of like a view port or viewing window. You can have a very large level which is way larger than the viewing screen so you need to control the placement of camera for the objects you place to remain visible. If what you have is a small single screen game (for purpose of learning programming a small screen game would be enough) then it should not matter at all. FYI this is a code block that deals with the placement of camera:

As previously said, most backgrounds come with predefined script. Refer to this example:

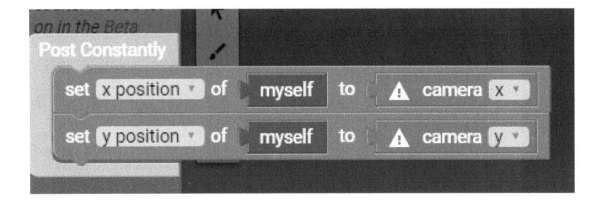

This actually keeps the background aligned with the camera. A recommended practice which is simple and straightforward is to center the camera on your main player object using this code block:

This way the main player object, the camera and the background will always be properly aligned.

Lesson 1 con't – the screen coordinates

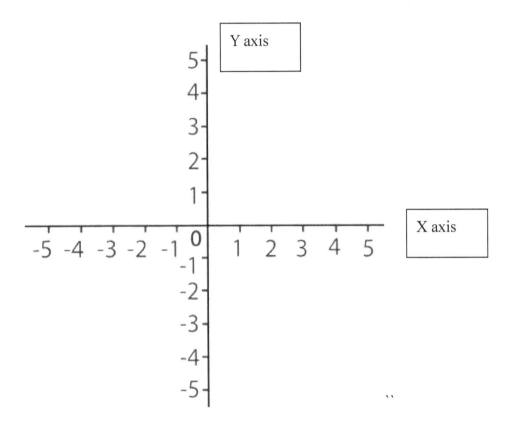

On a 2D screen, the coordinates are based on a system of

X and Y. This system is known as the Cartesian coordinate

system, which has a pair of lines on a flat surface that

intersect at right angles.   The lines are axes and the point

at which they intersect is the origin.   The axes are laid

horizontally and vertically and are known as the x-axis and y-axis respectively.

A point with coordinates X and Y is X units to the right of the y axis and Y units up from the x axis. In the world of mathematics, it is possible for them to carry negative values. For game creation purpose, however, they should stay positive if they are to be visible on screen. For Gamefroot:

- When Y increases, an object is moving down, and vice versa.

- When X increases, an object is moving to the right, and vice versa.

Lesson 1 con't – the Marketplace

Drawing and creating game arts is a totally different discipline. For the sake of learning programming, we recommend that you use ready made artworks. Apart from third party opensource, you can use artworks from the Gamefroot marketplace. There are many free game assets available over there.

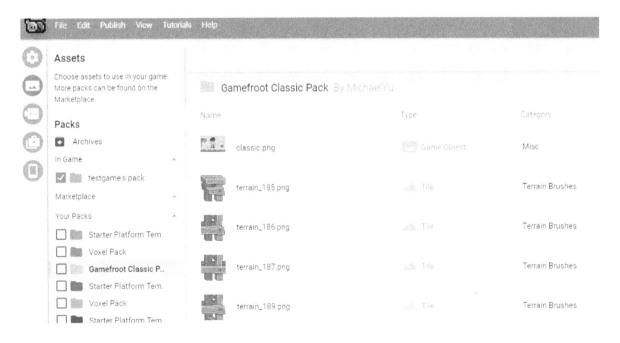

Assets are usually grouped into packs. One very popular

pack is the Gamefroot classic pack. You click to add the

pack to your game. The assets contained in the pack will

become available for use immediately.

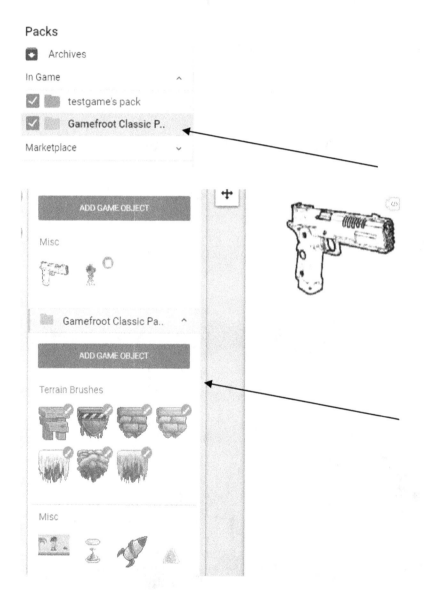

Copyright   2017   **The HobbyPRESS (Hong Kong)**.

Lesson 2– manipulating objects via code blocks

As p[previously said, you can actually use a code block under the script editor to resize an object. You can even position the object via code blocks. You can find these code blocks under Transform. You simply drag the blocks to the right and group them together, then key in the desired values. Because the size and position are manipulated programmatically, the changes are always reversible.

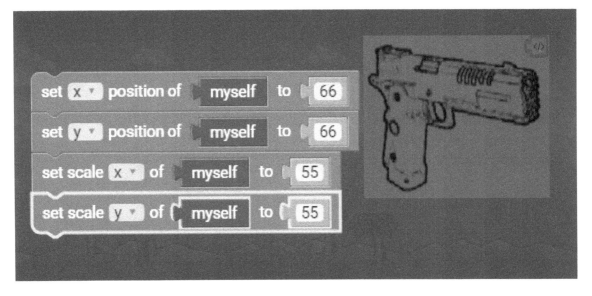

Myself refers to the current game object. You should try manipulating the values you use and see the effect. For example, if you set the scale to a value less than 1, you can make the object much smaller. x scale and Y scale can have different values!

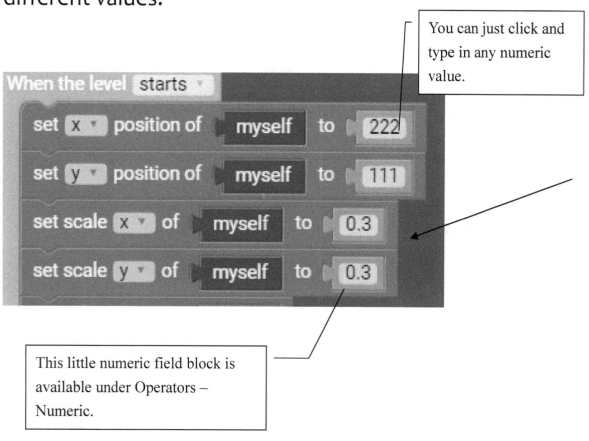

You can just click and type in any numeric value.

This little numeric field block is available under Operators – Numeric.

When you finish and switch back to Level Editor, make sure you name and save the script.

Script Properties

testmanipulate|

_____

Script Description

_____

Name	Type	Public	Default

This script doesn't contain any custom variables. Learn more about custom variables

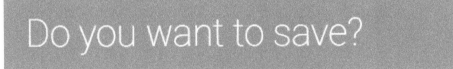

Do you want to save?

You have unsaved changes in the workspace, do you want to save them?

CANCEL   NO   SAVE

It should now be listed under Scripts. You can click Edit to edit it as needed.

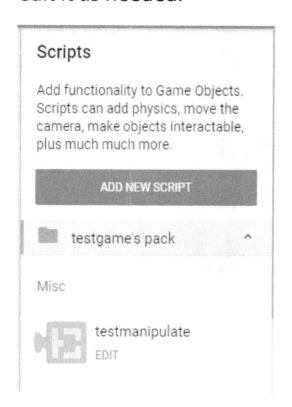

Now the script is tied to a particular object instance, but it will not run because there is no condition defined for it – it tells what to do, but it does not tell when to start doing... That's why you need to go to Events and pick an event condition for it:

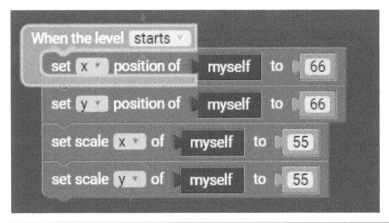

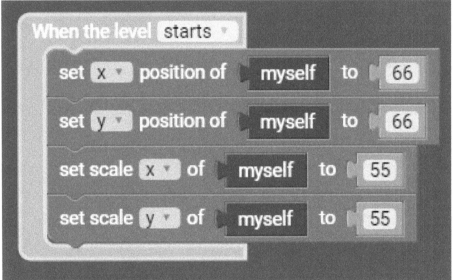

"When the level starts" is the event condition for the actions to be taken. Now when you click Play the script will run automatically.

"When the level starts" is a condition. When the level

switches (when you progress from one level to another) is another. All these can be adjusted on the code block. Each object has its own set of code blocks. You can have as many code blocks as you like for an object. In other words, multiple scripts can be tied to an object.

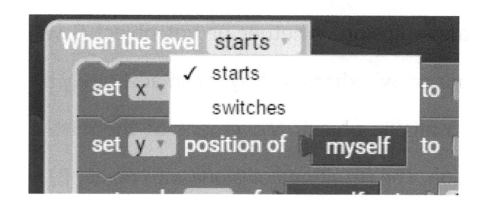

You need to know that all modern day programs are event driven. No actions will be taken unless some sort of event is taking place to trigger the actions. In an event driven environment, a program is structured in terms of events, with no preordered flow of control. Things do NOT start and proceed step by step. Instead, actions are associated with events, which will get invoked only when the corresponding event conditions are met (i.e. the event occurs). You do not know when these events will take place at design time. For example, object A has an action of shooting. This shooting action will not start UNLESS object B has an explosion. Whether or not object B will explode depends on whether the player can accurately hit object B with a missile object. Movement of the missile object is an action. The resulting collision (with object B) is an event. This event can trigger two sets of action: object B explodes and object A shoots. In Gamefroot, an event can trigger single or multiple actions. For an event to "take place", you can specify single or multiple conditions!

When there are multiple objects, you can use your mouse to drag and move each object to the desired location. If you need precise location and direction information of an object, sprite, navigate to Transform and choose the "Set X position of myself to" block.

You can also set object visibility programmatically. There is a block known as "set visibility of myself to true/false" which can be used to show or hide the object.

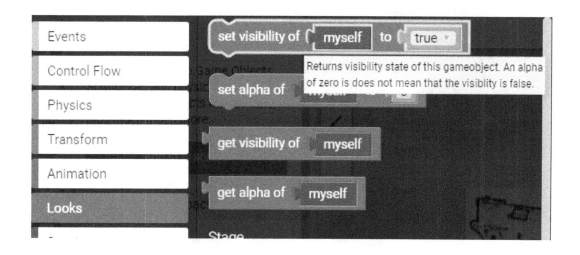

You can rotate an object via set rotation (under Transform):

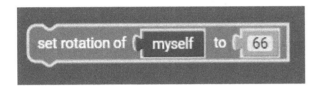

To produce movement, you need to repeatedly use this code block inside a loop. We will talk about loop in the next several sections.

Lesson 2 con't - processing user input

Different platforms accept different inputs. With Gamefroot, the most popular user input formats for desktop are mouse click and keyboard key press/release (they all belong to Events). For mobile, touch is rather common.

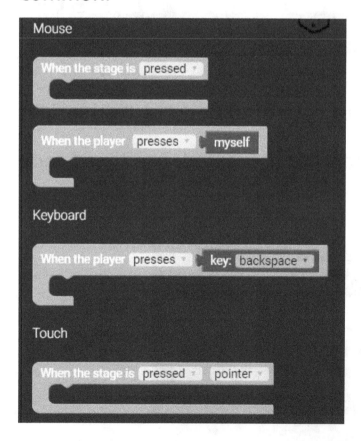

In any case, you need to tie an input event to a particular object. For example, you want the object to say hello to you when it is clicked ("pressed"). These are the code blocks to use ("create new textfield" is under Draw):

If you want the object to rotate 90 degrees to the right and say Hi when the spacebar is pressed, use these code blocks:

Note that you can further customize the text message display, such as the font color and the alignment. These code blocks are all available under Draw.

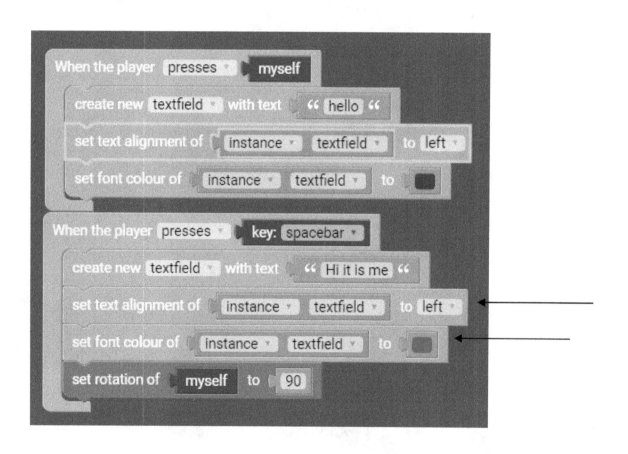

One thing you want to try is to fine tune the location where the text message is displayed. Under Transform you have the "set x position to" code block. You need to use it on "instance.textfield". You right click on any existing "instance.textfield" block and choose Duplicate, then drag the duplicated block into the "set x position to" code block. Do the same for y position.

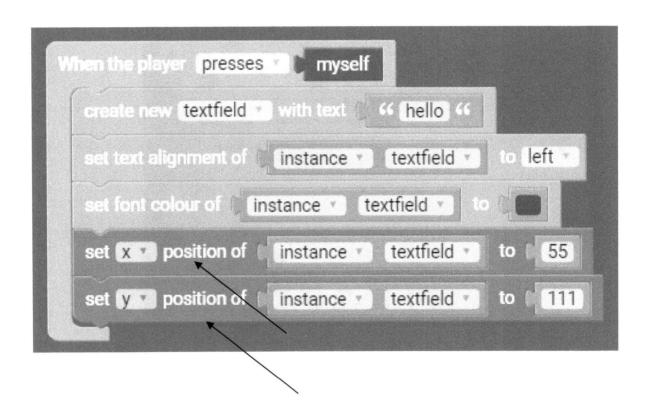

Lesson 2 con't – object interaction via messages

A program is all about interactions among objects! What we want you to achieve here is simple – when one object is receiving a user input, another object will give response in some way. With Gamefroot, this is possible via the use of message. Messages are under Events:

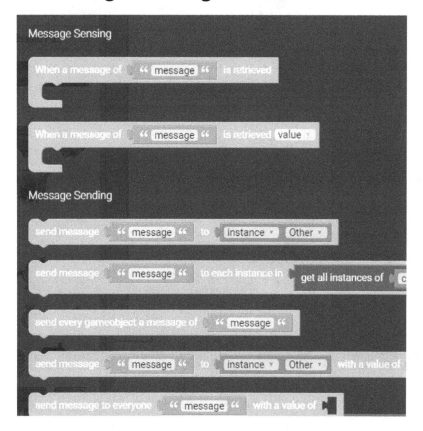

Messages can be sent (sending) and received (sensing). In this example, when one object receives a click, it will send out a message openly. Then when another object receives this message, it will rotate itself.

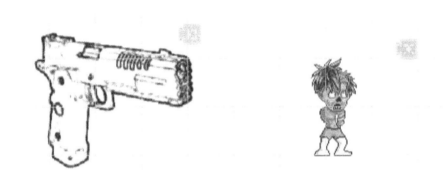

First you create an event on one object:

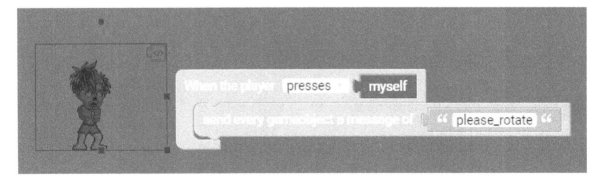

Script Properties

sendoutmessagewhenpressed

Script Description

Name	Type	Public	Default

This script doesn't contain any custom variables. Learn more about custom variables

When this object is pressed it will send out the "please_rotate" message. Now you configure the other object to listen to this particular message and rotate accordingly:

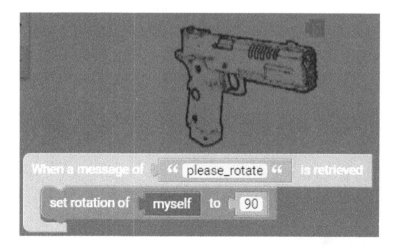

When it is pressed, it sends out a message.

Message received, then rotate.

Think of messages as a way for different objects to speak with each others. The message is kind of like a signal. You can define more messages for the objects to interact differently. You can create as many new messages as you like! As previously said, they are just signal - the meaning doesn't matter (but you can use a meaningful message to improve code readability).

Lesson 3 – if then else logic

You need an IF block to implement logical choices. IF is the most basic of all the control flow statements. It basically tells the program to execute a certain action (or a series of actions) only if a particular condition is evaluated to true. ELSE provides a secondary alternative path of execution when the IF condition evaluates to false.

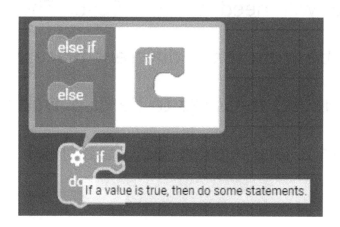

To summarize:

- IF   - IF some condition is true, perform an action;

otherwise do nothing.

- IF ELSE - IF some condition is true, perform an action; otherwise (ELSE) perform a different action.

- IF ELSE IF - IF some condition is true, perform an action; otherwise (ELSE IF) perform another evaluation.

You use IF when there is no alternative action. When there is alternative action, you will need to use ELSE. The condition to evaluate can be from many different places. For example, you want a HELLO message to be displayed when an object's X position is larger than 100, then this is what you will need:

From Transform:

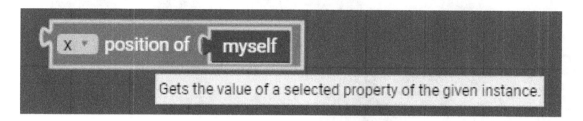

From Operators:

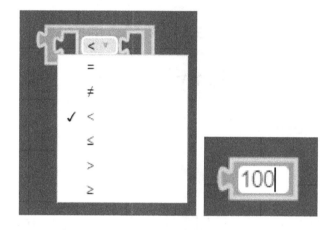

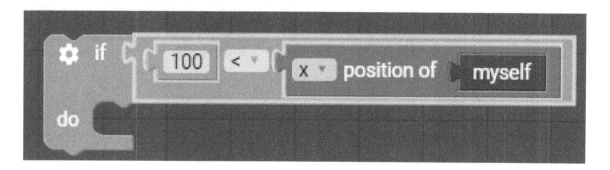

If you have several IF blocks and you plan them correctly, they may function exactly the same as having multiple ELSEs... Just remember, the evaluation would always go from top to bottom (i.e. sequentially).

Now you want to change this to an IF ELSE which is going to say "Oh god" if the X position is below 100. This is what you are going to need:

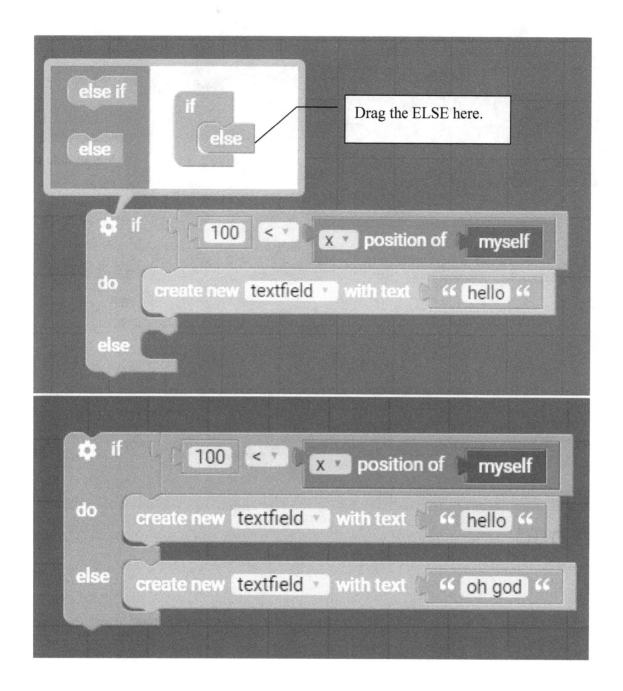

Drag the ELSE here.

This is how you may test out the entire IF structure:

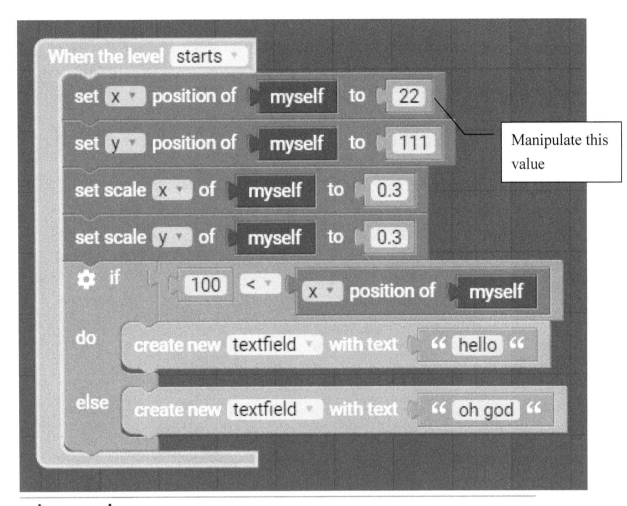

When the level [starts ▾]

  set [x ▾] position of [myself] to [22]

  set [y ▾] position of [myself] to [111]

  set scale [x ▾] of [myself] to [0.3]

  set scale [y ▾] of [myself] to [0.3]

  ⚙ if [100] [< ▾] [[x ▾] position of [myself]]

  do create new [textfield ▾] with text [" hello "]

  else create new [textfield ▾] with text [" oh god "]

Manipulate this value

oh god

Lesson 3 con't – and VS or

If the condition to evaluate has multiple elements that must exist together (AND) or individually (OR), you need to make use of the Boolean block under Operators. These blocks can be plugged into the IF block for defining multiple conditions.

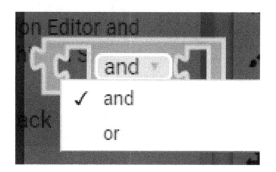

For example, to allow the object to say "Yeah" when both X and Y are larger than 100:

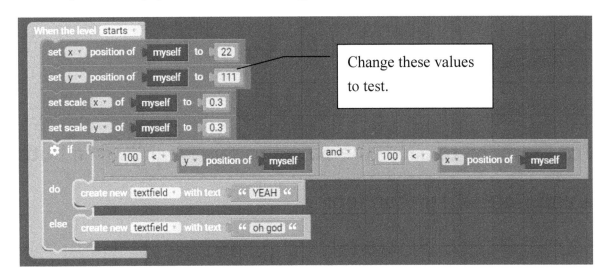

Now you may perform testing:

Change these values to test.

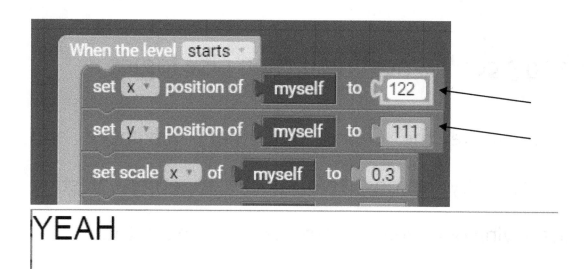

YEAH

Lesson 3 con't – nesting if then else logics

You can make the entire logic more advanced and complicated by nesting two blocks together. Nesting means having one type of instruction within another.

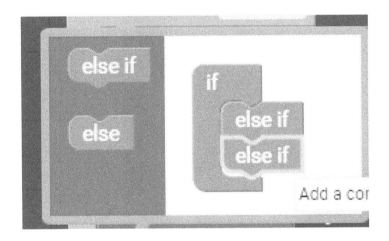

It is technically okay to have one or more IF/ELSE instructions within other IF/ELSE instructions. HOWEVER, when nesting goes too deep a level the entire block can become quite confusing to read and interpret.

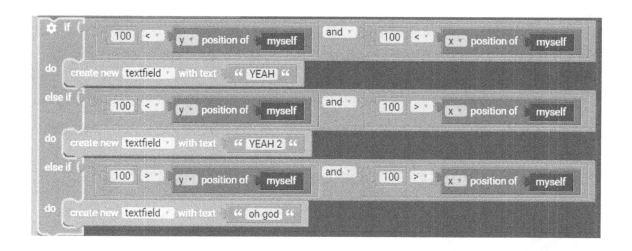

In theory you can nest more levels. It is entirely up to you on how to work out the logic, just that you need to make sure you don't make things too complicated...

Lesson 3 con't – other control flow measures

There are two code blocks that may be useful. The one below will trigger the code block it contains after a certain time duration has passed.

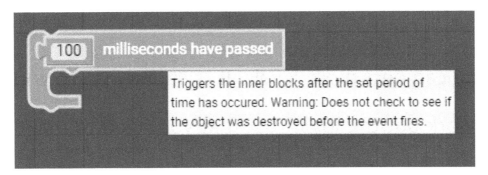

This one allows you to move to another level if you have multiple game levels defined.

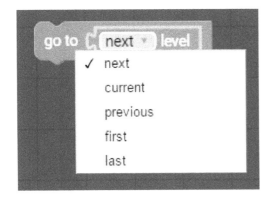

"When the level starts" is a very useful event condition. It kickstarts actions whenever the game level is started.

"When the level switches" is a condition where you are about to end the current level and go to another level.

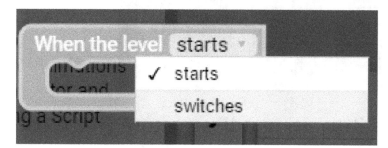

Constantly is very useful – if you want an event condition to be repeatedly monitored you will need to use it.

Remember this code block? This block is using a When structure.

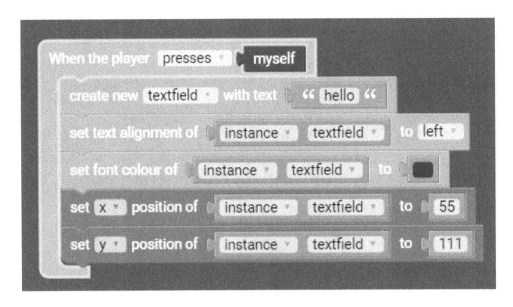

If you want to change it to using a IF structure (for more flexibility), you will need to modify it to use Constantly. You cannot just plug it into Constantly (by doing so you will need to change it to an IF structure first).

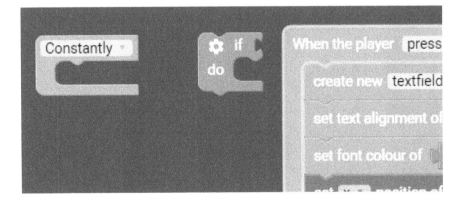

We also want you to change the condition. Instead of pressing, the condition will be met whenever the mouse cursor is moved to the same position as the object. You are going to need these:

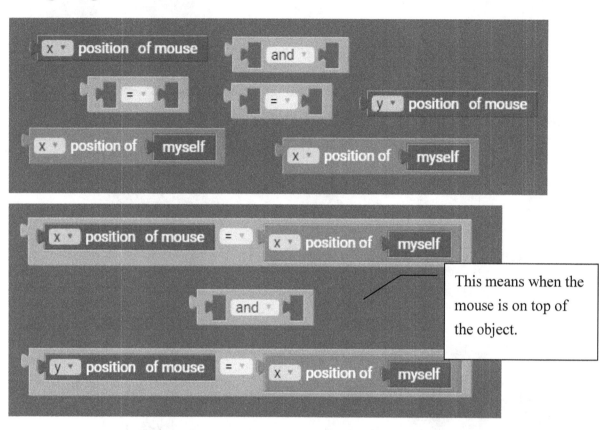

This means when the mouse is on top of the object.

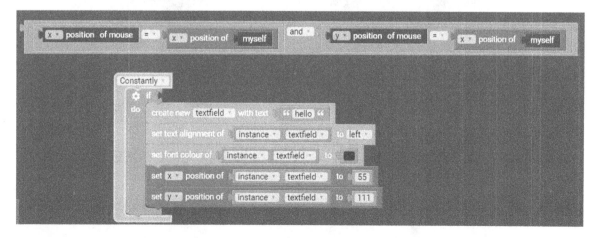

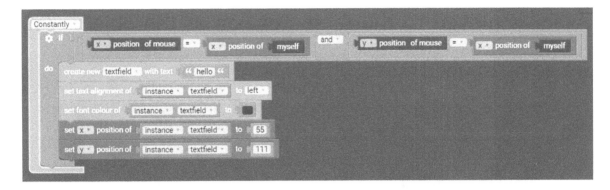

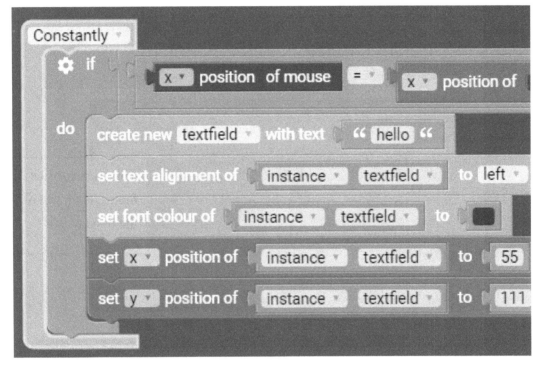

Now if you click Play and try, you will find out that the text

message will not get displayed. This is because it is very

difficult for you to move the mouse to a position so

precise that both X and Y can equal those of the object. For the logic to work, you need to play with the condition and probably loosen it a bit (for example, use < instead of =, use OR instead of AND):

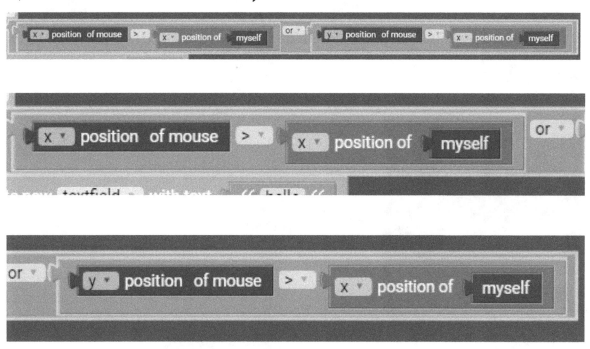

Now the text will get displayed, but you cannot tell if Constantly is working since the text is sitting still on the screen for good.

To be able to find out if Constantly is repeatedly evaluating the condition, change the font color to a random color so you will see some differences in the screen output (every time an evaluation is made a different color will be generated). The random color block is under Operators – Colour:

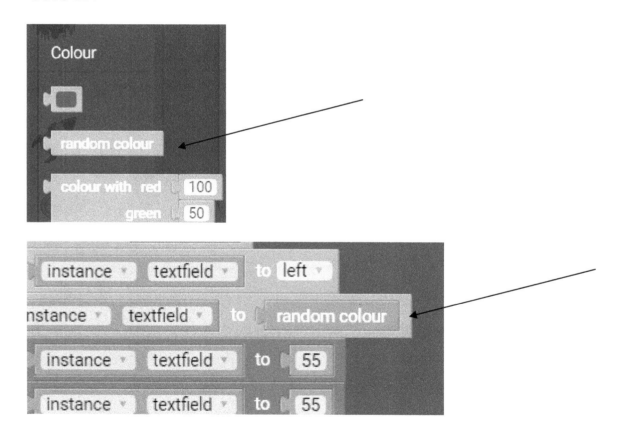

Copyright 2017 **The HobbyPRESS (Hong Kong)**. All rights reserved.

Lesson 4 - loop

A very important control logic you need to know is loop. A loop basically repeats things until a particular condition is met. A repeat loop is the most common form of loop in Gamefroot. This one lets you specify the number of times to repeat (you know in advance how many times you want the loop runs):

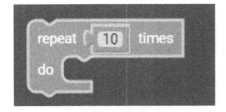

The following code block allows you to repeat or terminate some actions until a condition is met.

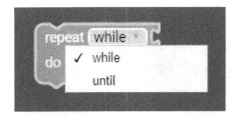

You will find loop useful if you want to produce movement. Say you want an object to keep moving to the right until it hits another object. You will use "repeat... 55 times". You need to keep incrementing X by 1:

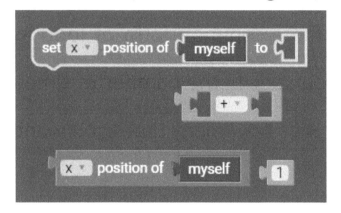

This basically says the new X equals current X plus 1.

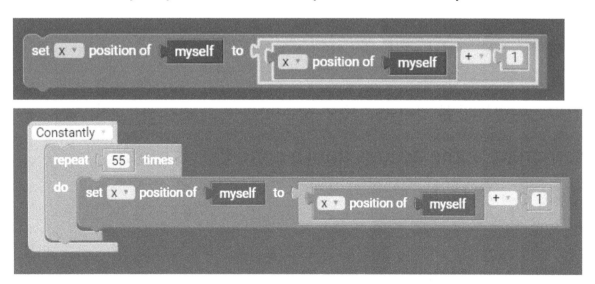

With this code block, the change X position action is being

repeated and repeated for 55 times.

Now if you want the loop to be more predictable, you should reorganize the code by first specifying a starting value for X. You should also set an IF condition which allows the loop to stop if a condition is met (such as if X exceeds a certain value). The break out of loop block is for quitting the loop.

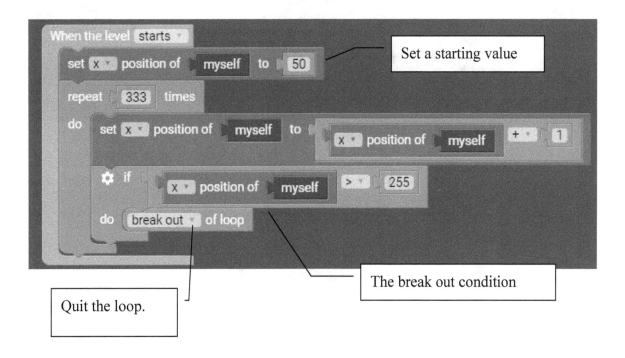

Set a starting value

The break out condition

Quit the loop.

If the movement is too fast, you can add a wait period before movement. You can do so using the "xxx mill seconds have passed" code block.

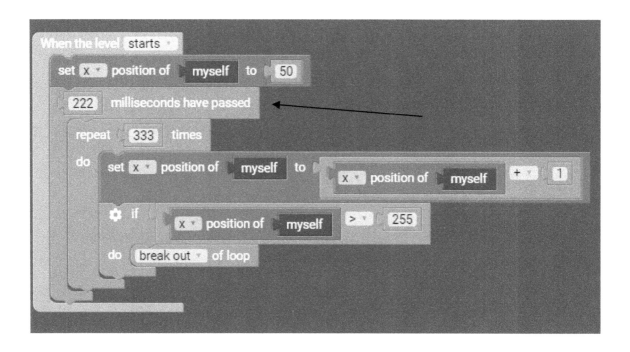

Lesson 4 con't – implementing movement control

Now you want to implement movement control so that the object can move according to the arrow key pressed. To move to the left/right for 10 pixels when the left/right arrow is pressed:

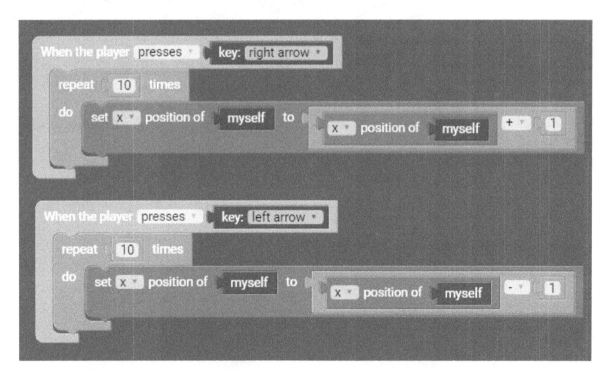

Copyright   2017

To move to up/down for 10 pixels when the up/down arrow is pressed, you need to manipulate the Y position instead:

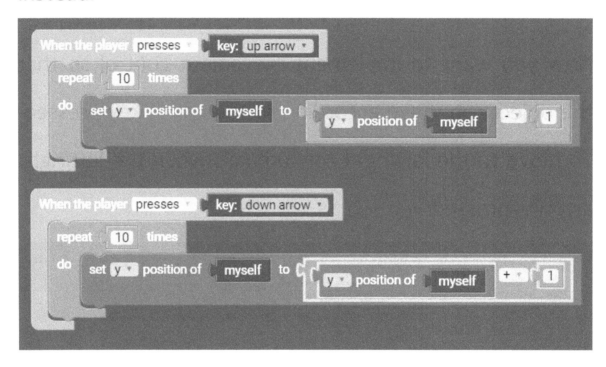

Now you have learnt the basics. In our advanced series books you will learn more advance coding concepts and techniques.

END OF BOOK

Please email your questions and comments to admin@Tomorrowskills.com.

www.ingramcontent.com/pod-product-compliance
Lightning Source LLC
Chambersburg PA
CBHW060203060326
40690CB00018B/4235